COLOR YOURSELF INSPIRED

Women's Bible Study

COLORING JOURNAL

Cover illustration: Emma Segal

Published by Barbour Books, an imprint of Barbour Publishing, Inc., P.O. Box 719, Uhrichsville, OH 44683, www.barbourbooks.com

Our mission is to publish and distribute inspirational products offering exceptional value and biblical encouragement to the masses.

 Member of the
Evangelical Christian
Publishers Association

Printed in the United States of America.

COLOR YOURSELF INSPIRED

Women's Bible Study Coloring Journal

Jessie Fioritto

BARBOUR BOOKS
An Imprint of Barbour Publishing, Inc.

Bible Study Topic:
GOD'S POWER

Read: EPHESIANS 1 AND 2

Key Scripture:

"For by grace you have been saved through faith; and that not of yourselves, it is the gift of God."

EPHESIANS 2:8 NASB

Life Application:

God will take whatever we give Him—our weaknesses, our poor decisions, our sin—and He will do something new. Our God is a God of second chances. He will always extend a do-over to anyone who calls on His name.

Reflect:

Do you need to experience the grace of second chances?

What do you need to give to God today?

Even before the world was created God chose me.
Ephesian 1:10-11 And this is the plan: At the right time he will
bring everything together under the authority of Christ Everything in Heaven
and Earth. Furthermore because we are united with Christ we
have recieved an inheritance from God for he chose us in advance
and he makes everything work out according to HIS plan. What
this was speaking to me is he has plans for me and they will
come to pass in his time. With that I need to daily
Surrender to his will and Surrender my broken heart to him
and trust him. When I thought I heard I need to just
trust it any for now because all this is driving me crazy
- God is to be #1 above anything and everything else.
Ephesian 2:10 For we are God's masterpiece. He has created
us anew in Christ Jesus so we can do the good things he
planned for us long ago. I am his masterpiece he's constantly
working on me for his purpose. It because hurt at times but
its for his glory and in the end I know I will be
thankful. Being made into the image of Christ hims!
And show me who or where I need to make and
God please heal my heart because its broken.

Pray:

Father God, You are the God of second chances. You are always faithful to offer me a
fresh start. Your mercies are new every morning. Thank You for changing my life through
the power of Your heavenly pardon. Amen.

Bible Study Topic:
REST IN HIS PEACE

Read: John 14:15-31

Key Scripture:

"Peace I leave with you; my peace I give to you. Not as the world gives do I give to you. Let not your hearts be troubled, neither let them be afraid."
John 14:27 ESV

Life Application:

Jesus doesn't offer us the same recycled promises the world can never fulfill. Through Jesus' sacrifice on the cross, we have peace with God, ourselves, and others. We have security from our fears and forgiveness for our sins.

Reflect:

Are you living in the peace of God?

Are there fears in your life that you haven't released to His capable hands?

John 14:2 - There is more than enough room in my Fathers home if this were not so would I told you that I am going to prepare a place for you? When everything is ready I will come and get you so that you will always be with me where I am and you know the way to where I'm going. (This brings me comfort to know that he will be back for me to spend eternity with him, he told the disciples that but it's also a promise to us as believers.

I have been long in God's peace I tought myself that I am but the reality is that I am broken down right now and truly and I have not fully gave that part of myself to my God. I have fears and bitterness and resentment about the Fabian situation and I need to give fully surrender and live in peace but it's so hard. ⚘

Pray:

God, I'm so grateful for the peace that flows from my relationship with You. My eternity is secure with You, so I need not fear this world. Thank You for Jesus, who restored peace between my Creator and me. Amen.

Bible Study Topic:
GOD'S POWER

Read: Psalm 46

Key Scripture:

"Be still, and know that I am God."
Psalm 46:10 ESV

Life Application:

We think we're the glue that holds everything together—that nothing could succeed without our effort—and we're indispensable. But God is really the one who holds it all in place, and sometimes He wants us to be still and watch Him work.

Reflect:

When was the last time you stopped everything to worship God, just because He's God? Do you need to set time aside in your busy schedule to "be still" with God?

_____

_____

_____

_____

_____

_____

_____

_____

_____

_____

_____

_____

_____

_____

_____

Pray:

God, at times my life feels like an endless cycle of multitasking—my attention never fully on one thing. Help me quiet my hands and my mind and bask in the knowledge that You are God. You've got this! Amen.

Bible Study Topic:
GARMENTS OF VIRTUE

Read: COLOSSIANS 3

Key Scripture:

Clothe yourselves with compassion, kindness, humility, gentleness and patience. Bear with each other and forgive one another if any of you has a grievance against someone. Forgive as the Lord forgave you. And over all these virtues put on love, which binds them all together in perfect unity.

COLOSSIANS 3:12-14 NIV

Life Application:

Some people have crafted a trademark look. Their clothes define their personality, and at first glance you know something significant about them. As the redeemed of Jesus, our "look" should be characterized by His virtues.

Reflect:

Do people around you see Jesus through the virtues you wear?

Which virtues are lacking in your heart?

_____

_____

_____

_____

_____

_____

_____

_____

_____

_____

_____

_____

_____

_____

_____

Pray:

Lord, I want to wear love, compassion, kindness, humility, gentleness, and patience. Help me develop a heart that is beautiful to You. Keep my eyes focused on the things above, things of eternal value to Your Kingdom. Amen.

Bible Study Topic:
PERFECT LOVE

Read: 1 John 4

Key Scripture:

There is no fear in love. But perfect love drives out fear, because fear has to do with punishment. The one who fears is not made perfect in love.

1 John 4:18 NIV

Life Application:

Fear and love cannot coexist. If we truly believe God's perfect love for us, we will live in the peace, rest, and security that we desire. The more deeply we understand God's love for us, the more fully we will love others.

Reflect:

What fears bind you today?

How can the truth of God's love for you silence those fears?

_____

_____

_____

_____

_____

_____

_____

_____

_____

_____

_____

_____

_____

_____

_____

Pray:

God, reveal the depth of Your love for me. Drive out my fears with the consuming power of Your love. Help me love those around me, not through my own ability, but because You first loved me. Amen.

Bible Study Topic:
THE NEW YOU

Read: 2 Corinthians 5

Key Scripture:

Therefore, if anyone is in Christ, he is a new creation. The old has passed away; behold, the new has come.

2 Corinthians 5:17 ESV

Life Application:

Out with the old. In with the new. When you have Jesus, you're no longer stuck living the way you used to live, doing what you did before. You're a beautiful new creation. The old you is dead. Now you're truly alive.

Reflect:

Have you ever reverted to your old ways of doing things after you came to Jesus?
In what ways does knowing you're a new creature in Christ change you?

_____

_____

_____

_____

_____

_____

_____

_____

_____

_____

_____

_____

_____

_____

Pray:

Jesus, You've wiped away every sin I've ever committed. You've changed me, renewed me, created me again. Like an artist who reuses an old canvas, You've painted over the old with something beautiful. Amen.

Bible Study Topic:
GOD CARES

Read: 1 Peter 5

Key Scripture:

Cast all your anxiety on him because he cares for you.
1 Peter 5:7 NIV

Life Application:

God cares about you. His shoulders are wide enough to bear your burdens, and He wants to lift them all from your back. He asks for *all* your anxiety so He can restore you and make you strong and steadfast.

Reflect:

Did you know that the God of the universe cares about the worries that wear you down?

Have you released all your anxiety to God so He can strengthen your faith?

_____

_____

_____

_____

_____

_____

_____

_____

_____

_____

_____

_____

_____

_____

_____

_____

Pray:

God of everything, thank You for caring about me. I'm not insignificant to You. Jesus, I'm tired. Please take my fears and worries and replace them with a faith that is firmly rooted in You. Restore my soul. Amen.

Bible Study Topic:
FORGIVEN

Read: Matthew 6:5-15

Key Scripture:

"And forgive us our debts, as we also have forgiven our debtors."
Matthew 6:12 esv

Life Application:

We are forgiven! God has taken the dark blot of our sin and wiped it clean with Jesus' blood. And because we have been forgiven, we, too, can forgive. Just remember God's mercy toward you, and offer it to others.

Reflect:

Is there someone that you need to forgive?

How does unforgiveness hinder our fellowship with God?

_____

_____

_____

_____

_____

_____

_____

_____

_____

_____

_____

_____

_____

_____

_____

Pray:

Jesus, I'm so grateful that You died on the cross so my sins could be forgiven. When someone wrongs me, help me remember that I am not perfect, but You showed me mercy. Give me grace to forgive others. Amen.

Bible Study Topic:
PLEASING PRAYERS

Read: Psalm 141

Key Scripture:

Let my prayer be counted as incense before you, and the lifting up of my hands as the evening sacrifice!

Psalm 141:2 esv

Life Application:

God delights in our prayers. He wants to hear from us. In the tabernacle, the evening sacrifice contained incense; its sweet aroma ascended to heaven, just as our prayers do, and pleased the Lord.

Reflect:

Do you spend time each day talking to God in prayer?

Have you considered that your prayers bring pleasure to God?

_____

_____

_____

_____

_____

_____

_____

_____

_____

_____

_____

_____

_____

Pray:

God, I'm sorry if I have neglected my prayer life. Help me reevaluate my priorities and set aside time to talk with You. I'm in awe that my prayers please You. May my prayers rise like the scent of sweet incense. Amen.

Bible Study Topic:
WORD OF LIFE

Read: 1 John 1

Key Scripture:

This we proclaim concerning the Word of life. The life appeared; we have seen it and testify to it, and we proclaim to you the eternal life, which was with the Father and has appeared to us.

1 John 1:1-2 NIV

Life Application:

Jesus—the Word of life—is the living proclamation of God's gift of eternal life to us. The Greek meaning for *word* includes "revelation." Jesus came to earth to reveal the Father. Stand in awe for a moment that God wants to be known.

Reflect:

Have you accepted God's gift of eternal life?

In what ways does Jesus, God's living Word, show the Father's love for us?

_____

_____

_____

_____

_____

_____

_____

_____

_____

_____

_____

_____

_____

_____

_____

Pray:

Father God, when I feel that You are far away from my care-worn life, I have to remind myself that You want me to know You. Your infinite love was revealed in Jesus. Thank You, Father, for loving me. Amen.

Bible Study Topic:
BEAUTIFUL INSIDE

Read: 1 Samuel 16:1–13; Psalm 139

Key Scripture:

"For the Lord sees not as man sees: man looks on the outward appearance, but the Lord looks on the heart."

1 Samuel 16:7 esv

Life Application:

We go to great lengths for pleasing aesthetics. We pour thousands of dollars into plastic surgery and home renovations. God loves beauty, too. Just look at His breathtaking handiwork. But He is more concerned with rejuvenating our hearts.

Reflect:

Does God see the beautiful traits of faith, love, and hope in your heart?

How can you spend more time cultivating virtues that are pleasing to God?

_____

_____

_____

_____

_____

_____

_____

_____

_____

_____

_____

_____

_____

Pray:

Heavenly Father, I echo David's prayer: "Search me, O God, and know my heart! Try me and know my thoughts! And see if there be any grievous way in me, and lead me in the way everlasting!" (Psalm 139:23-24 ESV). Amen.

Bible Study Topic:
TRUST IN GOD

Read: John 14:1–14

Key Scripture:

"Let not your hearts be troubled. Believe in God; believe also in me."
John 14:1 ESV

Life Application:

We live in a troubling world filled with gut-wrenching crime, disease, and poverty. But Jesus reassures His followers, "Do not let your hearts be troubled." How comforting to know He is our hope for a better future.

Reflect:

Do you trust God with both your present circumstances *and* your future?

What prevents you from trusting God with certain areas of your life?

_____

_____

_____

_____

_____

_____

_____

_____

_____

_____

_____

_____

_____

_____

Pray:

God, You created all things and hold the earth in Your hands. You are able. You are wise. You are trustworthy. Thank You for sending us Jesus, who is the truth, the life, and the only way to You. Amen.

Bible Study Topic:
GOD IS MY SHEPHERD

Read: ISAIAH 40

Key Scripture:

He tends his flock like a shepherd: He gathers the lambs in his arms and carries them close to his heart; he gently leads those that have young.

ISAIAH 40:11 NIV

Life Application:

A shepherd defends his flock from predators, carefully leads them to green pastures and clear water, and lifts the young and injured onto his strong shoulders. God is our tender and gentle shepherd who carries us when we're weak.

Reflect:

Do you see God as gentle and tender?

Have there been times in your life when God carried you close to His heart?

_____

_____

_____

_____

_____

_____

_____

_____

_____

_____

_____

_____

_____

_____

Pray:

Father, You are mighty and powerful, yet compassionate and nurturing. Give me rest and peace in the knowledge that You shepherd me through the dangers and trials of life. You protect, provide for, and sustain me. Amen.

Bible Study Topic:
HOPE FOR THE FUTURE

Read: ROMANS 5

Key Scripture:

We rejoice in our sufferings, knowing that suffering produces endurance, and endurance produces character, and character produces hope, and hope does not put us to shame, because God's love has been poured into our hearts through the Holy Spirit.
ROMANS 5:3-5 ESV

Life Application:

Without hope people wither and harden—they throw up their hands in bleak surrender. But as believers we have eternal hope in Jesus. No matter what we are suffering through, our hope rests on His promise of eternal life.

Reflect:

Have you ever lost hope in your future?

Have you placed your hope in the wrong source?

_____

_____

_____

_____

_____

_____

_____

_____

_____

_____

_____

_____

_____

_____

_____

Pray:

Lord, thank You for the hope of a glorious, eternal future with You. Please give me strength to bear up under trial because You promise a harvest of perseverance, character, and hope through difficult times. Amen.

Bible Study Topic:
ASK FOR WISDOM

Read: JAMES 1

Key Scripture:

If any of you lacks wisdom, let him ask God, who gives generously to all without reproach, and it will be given him.

JAMES 1:5 ESV

Life Application:

Have you ever spent hours weighing the pros and cons and still felt unsure about your decision? We have the Holy Spirit and God's Word to guide us. Ask God to teach you and give you wisdom, and He will.

Reflect:

Are you facing a decision or situation that requires wisdom?

Has the Holy Spirit, through God's Word, ever taught you something you couldn't have known otherwise?

_____

_____

_____

_____

_____

_____

_____

_____

_____

_____

_____

_____

_____

Pray:

God, teach me something today. You didn't leave me here to figure life out on my own. Give me wisdom and discernment in my decisions. Reveal Yourself to me. Show me Your plan for my life. Amen.

Bible Study Topic:
GOD CAN

Read: 1 John 5

Key Scripture:

This is the confidence we have in approaching God: that if we ask anything according to his will, he hears us. And if we know that he hears us—whatever we ask—we know that we have what we asked of him.

1 John 5:14–15 NIV

Life Application:

God hears our prayers, but we often limit Him to what we think He can do. We are His beloved; He longs to give us good things. Ask according to His will. Please Him with obedience. Know that He hears. And see what He will do.

Reflect:

Have you ever prayed for something with the wrong motives?

Have you limited the truth of 1 John 5:14-15?

_____

_____

_____

_____

_____

_____

_____

_____

_____

_____

_____

_____

_____

_____

_____

_____

_____

Pray:

Heavenly Father, I know that You hear my prayers. Forgive me for the times I've asked things with selfish motives. Your plan is so much bigger than I can imagine. Give me patience to trust Your answers to my prayers. Amen.

Bible Study Topic:
INTO THE LIGHT

Read: 1 John 1

Key Scripture:

God is light, and in him is no darkness at all.

1 John 1:5 esv

Life Application:

Imagine the best person you know, the kindest and most loving. Now magnify that goodness a million times and you'll begin to perceive God's lovingkindness. God has no hidden agenda or selfish motives. He is pure light.

Reflect:

Have you ever questioned God's goodness toward you?

What do you love most about each side of this truth: "God is light"; "in him is no darkness"?

_____

_____

_____

_____

_____

_____

_____

_____

_____

_____

_____

_____

_____

_____

_____

Pray:

God, You are light. Bright and cleansing light that annihilates the darkness. Light always wins because darkness has no choice but to scatter in its presence. Forgive me for questioning Your goodness when You have nothing to hide. Amen.

Bible Study Topic:
THE SPIRIT SPEAKS FOR US

Read: ROMANS 8

Key Scripture:

The Spirit himself intercedes for us with groanings too deep for words.
ROMANS 8:26 ESV

Life Application:

Have you ever felt like you were without allies and no one had your back? Jesus sent the Holy Spirit as our helper. We're not in this alone. Even if we don't know what to pray, the Holy Spirit intercedes for us.

Reflect:

How does knowing that the Holy Spirit intercedes for you change your outlook?

Have you ever tried to pray but were unable to form the words for yourself?

Pray:

God, I never need to feel alone, misunderstood, or outcast. You send me help to strengthen me when I'm weak and to speak on my behalf when I don't have the words. Your love and provision amaze me. Amen.

Bible Study Topic:
THE VALUE OF VIRTUE

Read: Proverbs 31:10-31

Key Scripture:

A wife of noble character who can find? She is worth far more than rubies.
Proverbs 31:10 NIV

Life Application:

Set your heart on becoming a woman of character and you will be of great worth to those around you—more valuable than rubies. We may not be able to significantly alter our looks or our smarts, but we can mold our character.

Reflect:

Have you ever based your self-worth on things you can't change about yourself?
How can you become a woman of noble character?

_____

_____

_____

_____

_____

_____

_____

_____

_____

_____

_____

_____

_____

_____

Pray:

Lord, You created me just as You wanted me to be. Cultivate Your virtues in my life. Teach me to be loving, merciful, kind, gentle, faithful, and forgiving. Let my value to Your Kingdom be greater than precious jewels. Amen.

Bible Study Topic:
PRAY FIRST

Read: Psalm 34

Key Scripture:

I sought the Lord, and he answered me and delivered me from all my fears.
Psalm 34:4 ESV

Life Application:

Why should we waste our time worrying when we can pray? Fear devours our lives and erodes our joy. So bring your concerns before the Lord. He will answer your prayers. You just have to ask.

Reflect:

Is prayer your first line of defense against worry. . .or your last?

Has God ever answered your prayer but not with the answer you wanted? How did you respond?

_____

_____

_____

_____

_____

_____

_____

_____

_____

_____

_____

_____

_____

_____

Pray:

God, You gave us this amazing way to come into Your holy presence and seek comfort, wisdom, and guidance from the God of the universe! Nudge me to pray first rather than last. Amen.

Bible Study Topic:
GOD IS KIND

Read: ROMANS 2:1–16; ROMANS 5:8

Key Scripture:

God's kindness is intended to lead you to repentance.
ROMANS 2:4 NIV

Life Application:

It's love that God has for us. And His love is unlike any love that we've ever encountered. Rather than slapping us with divine judgment, God intends to woo us as a bridegroom with his bride—by His lovingkindness.

Reflect:

Have you ever questioned God's kindness, love, and good intentions for you?

How do God's patience, forbearance, and kindness lead us to repentance?

_____

_____

_____

_____

_____

_____

_____

_____

_____

_____

_____

_____

_____

_____

Pray:

God, thank You for being patient with me. Thank You for withholding the punishment I deserve and instead showing me measureless love and underserved kindness. You proved Your love by dying for me, a sinner. Amen.

Bible Study Topic:
GOD IS HERE

Read: Zephaniah 3

Key Scripture:

"The Lord your God is in your midst."
Zephaniah 3:17 ESV

Life Application:

God is here! In our midst. Through devastation and triumph. Our God doesn't recline in some faraway throne room, distanced from the reality we experience. He is sovereign and holy, but He is not aloof.

Reflect:

Have you ever felt that God was too distant to care about you?

Did you know that He delights in being with you?

Pray:

God, I praise Your name. You are mighty to save me. Your love consoles me. You didn't create us only to leave us. You dwell among us. You are here in my midst. Thank You for promising never to leave me. Amen.

Bible Study Topic:
THINK BEAUTIFUL THOUGHTS

Read: PHILIPPIANS 3–4

Key Scripture:

Whatever is true, whatever is noble, whatever is right, whatever is pure, whatever is lovely, whatever is admirable—if anything is excellent or praiseworthy—think about such things.

PHILIPPIANS 4:8 NIV

Life Application:

Poet Pablo Neruda wrote, "As if you were on fire from within. The moon lives in the lining of your skin." Moon glow is a reflection of the sun's light into the darkness. Kindle your inner fire for God—dwell on pure and lovely things.

Reflect:

Are your thoughts most often uplifting or destructive?

How can you better reflect Christ's love to others by thinking about pure and lovely things?

_____

_____

_____

_____

_____

_____

_____

_____

_____

_____

_____

_____

_____

Pray:

Jesus, set my heart on what is true, noble, pure, lovely, and admirable. Rid my mind of ugly thoughts—jealousy, pettiness, unforgiveness. Let Your light shine from within me to the dark world around me. Amen.

Bible Study Topic:
TOO BUSY FOR JESUS

Read: Luke 10:38-42

Key Scripture:

"Martha, Martha," the Lord answered, "you are worried and upset about many things, but few things are needed—or indeed only one. Mary has chosen what is better, and it will not be taken away from her."

Luke 10:41-42 NIV

Life Application:

Mary's heart was drawn to things not of this world, while Martha was distracted by dinner. Jesus wasn't criticizing Martha's hospitality. He was pointing her to the power and sufficiency of His Kingdom.

Reflect:

What is your top priority in life right now?

Are you distracted from God's greater plan by temporary things of this world?

_____

_____

_____

_____

_____

_____

_____

_____

_____

_____

_____

_____

_____

_____

_____

Pray:

Lord, You know my life is chaotic, busy, even crazy sometimes. But all that fades away when I spend time with You, my friend. Mary knew what she was doing, forsaking other things for You. Help me do the same. Amen.

Bible Study Topic:
TENDER SHEPHERD

Read: PSALM 23

Key Scripture:

The LORD is my shepherd; I shall not want. He makes me lie down in green pastures. He leads me beside still waters. He restores my soul.

PSALM 23:1-3 ESV

Life Application:

A rejuvenating day at the spa—worries slide away as you're cared for. God, too, offers tender ministrations for His weary lambs. Lying in green fields, beside calm pools. Restoration for not just your body, but your soul.

Reflect:

Is a tender shepherd consistent with your image of God?

How does this verse from Psalms change your view on God's care for you?

_____

_____

_____

_____

_____

_____

_____

_____

_____

_____

_____

_____

_____

Pray:

Heavenly Father, You offer rest for my body and new life for my soul. I'm so grateful for the loving provision You offer. I have no need to fear or want for anything, because You are my shepherd. Amen.

Bible Study Topic:
A MERCIFUL HEART

Read: MATTHEW 5

Key Scripture:

"Blessed are the merciful, for they shall receive mercy."
MATTHEW 5:7 ESV

Life Application:

Mercy over punishment. Not only are we spared the consequences of our actions, but Jesus took our lashes on His own back. Mercy is defined as active compassion, withholding just consequences. How can we, in turn, offer any less?

Reflect:

Have you ever shown mercy to someone who wronged you?

Do you believe that God can be both just and merciful?

_____

_____

_____

_____

_____

_____

_____

_____

_____

_____

_____

_____

_____

_____

Pray:

Lord Jesus, plant in me a merciful heart. You have forgiven every wrong I've ever committed. Beyond that, You were broken so I could be given mercy. Never let me forget Your compassion. Amen.

Bible Study Topic:
SOUL REST

Read: Matthew 11

Key Scripture:

"Come to me, all you who are weary and burdened, and I will give you rest. . . . For my yoke is easy and my burden is light."

Matthew 11:28, 30 NIV

Life Application:

Rest for the tired and oppressed—it's not too good to be true. Following Jesus can be difficult, but it will never be a burden. Jesus gently applies a balm of forgiveness, love, and acceptance—rest for your soul.

Reflect:

Is your soul heavy with guilt, anxiety, hopelessness, or anger?

How can something be difficult yet not burdensome?

_____

_____

_____

_____

_____

_____

_____

_____

_____

_____

_____

_____

_____

_____

_____

Pray:

Jesus, I take up Your yoke. You promise that by walking in obedience to You I will find rest—a light load to carry and freedom from oppression. You are my gentle and humble Shepherd King. Amen.

Bible Study Topic:
STANDING STRONG

Read: Psalm 119

Key Scripture:

Great peace have those who love your law, and nothing can make them stumble.
Psalm 119:165 NIV

Life Application:

God's Word is our offensive weapon. We must assiduously train to meet our enemy, Satan and his forces of darkness, on the spiritual battlefield where souls hang in the balance. Memorize God's Word. Speak life. Repel the enemy.

Reflect:

Have you applied God's Word to an area in your life where you're stumbling?

Do you regularly and intentionally memorize scripture?

_____

_____

_____

_____

_____

_____

_____

_____

_____

_____

_____

_____

_____

Pray:

God, You gave me Your life-breathed Word that is sharper than any two-edged sword and powerful to cut down my enemy. May Your words take root in my heart. May I never enter the battlegrounds defenseless against Satan. Amen.

Bible Study Topic:
TRUTH AND LOVE

Read: 2 John

Key Scripture:

Grace, mercy and peace from God the Father and from Jesus Christ, the Father's Son, will be with us in truth and love.

2 John 3 NIV

Life Application:

Truth and love are entwined in a beautiful symbiosis. As followers of Jesus, no longer motivated by mere sentiment or cold judgment, we are spurred to love because we have encountered the Truth face-to-face.

Reflect:

Have you ever acted in truth, but realized you needed to temper it with love?

Have you ever acted in love, but realized you needed to bolster it with truth?

_____

_____

_____

_____

_____

_____

_____

_____

_____

_____

_____

_____

_____

_____

Pray:

Heavenly Father, guide me along the path of truth and love You've called me to walk. Give me wisdom in applying both elements in every situation I encounter because neither extreme reflects You. Amen.

Bible Study Topic:
SPEAK LIFE

Read: EPHESIANS 3-4

Key Scripture:

Do not let any unwholesome talk come out of your mouths but only what is helpful for building others up according to their needs, that it may benefit those who listen.
EPHESIANS 4:29 NIV

Life Application:

Gossip floats on the air around us, but its poisonous cloud seldom bears positivity. One negative word can cut deeply and sever friendships. Resolve to speak life—build up, encourage, and uplift.

Reflect:

Have you ever wounded someone with something you've said?

Have you ever considered whether what you were about to say was helpful or beneficial?

Pray:

Jesus, guard my tongue. It can spread death or life, depending on how I use it. I want to be a person who speaks life. You are the way, the truth, and the life. Put Your words on my lips daily. Amen.

Bible Study Topic:
HOPE IN GLORY

Read: 2 Corinthians 4

Key Scripture:

For our light and momentary troubles are achieving for us an eternal glory that far outweighs them all.

2 Corinthians 4:17 NIV

Life Application:

We live with the hope of eternal glory. That's the secret to bearing the hard things we encounter in this world. Sin has overrun God's perfect creation here on earth, but glory awaits us when we see Him again.

Reflect:

Does eternity with Christ give you hope when disappointment or devastation assault you? In what ways might remembering that this life is momentary change the way you live?

_____

_____

_____

_____

_____

_____

_____

_____

_____

_____

_____

_____

_____

Pray:

Father God, I'm so grateful that I have hope in the promise of an eternal future with You. The troubles of this world just don't seem as oppressive when cast against the glory we will experience forever. Amen.

Bible Study Topic:
GOD IS GREATER

Read: 1 John 3

Key Scripture:

This is how we know that we belong to the truth and how we set our hearts at rest in his presence: If our hearts condemn us, we know that God is greater than our hearts, and he knows everything.

1 John 3:19-20 NIV

Life Application:

Who needs critics when our own self-talk can be so vicious? God is greater than our hyperjudgmental hearts. And He longs to put us at ease in His presence because we're redeemed. Believe this truth instead of the enemy's lies.

Reflect:

Does your heart ever condemn you (even if you deserve it)?

Have you ever avoided God because of guilt or feelings of inadequacy?

_____

_____

_____

_____

_____

_____

_____

_____

_____

_____

_____

_____

_____

_____

Pray:

God, forgive me for thinking that I need to run from Your presence like Adam and Eve when I don't feel good enough. Allow my heart to rest at ease in Your company because You are greater than my condemning heart. Amen.

Bible Study Topic:
WHAT LOVE IS

Read: 1 Corinthians 13

Key Scripture:

Love is patient, love is kind. It does not envy, it does not boast, it is not proud. It does not dishonor others, it is not self-seeking, it is not easily angered, it keeps no record of wrongs. Love does not delight in evil but rejoices with the truth. It always protects, always trusts, always hopes, always perseveres.

1 Corinthians 13:4–7 NIV

Life Application:

Our love can't be weighed by the words we throw around. Love propels us to get up and *do* something. Even if we come up short of a 1 Corinthians kind of love, God's love for us will *always* measure up.

Reflect:

In what ways do you love (or not love) those around you with your actions?

Did you know that because God is love, all of the qualities listed in 1 Corinthians are reflective of God?

_____

_____

_____

_____

_____

_____

_____

_____

_____

_____

_____

_____

_____

_____

Pray:

God, please help me to love more like You do. Often my desires are selfish and my patience and kindness run thin. But You love me so perfectly that I want to give that kind of love away. Amen.

Bible Study Topic:
CHANGED

Read: ROMANS 12

Key Scripture:

Do not conform to the pattern of this world, but be transformed by the renewing of your mind.

ROMANS 12:2 NIV

Life Application:

Stand out. Think differently. Act differently. Be changed because you now function with the mind of Christ. The world says to please yourself and mind your own business. But Jesus says help the hurting and wretched.

Reflect:

Is it obvious in your life that you don't conform to the world's pattern?

How has your thinking changed since you've encountered Jesus?

_____

_____

_____

_____

_____

_____

_____

_____

_____

_____

_____

_____

_____

_____

Pray:

Lord Jesus, I met You and everything changed. The blinders were ripped from my eyes, and I see this world clearly. I know there's more than this wearying place in my future. Thank You, Jesus, for saving my soul! Amen.

Bible Study Topic:
GO DEEPER

Read: PHILIPPIANS 1-2

Key Scripture:

And this is my prayer: that your love may abound more and more in knowledge and depth of insight.

PHILIPPIANS 1:9 NIV

Life Application:

Want your love for others to deepen? Get to know Jesus better. Once you encounter the amazing love of Jesus, you can't help but see everyone around you through His filter—as His family. And Jesus wants them redeemed.

Reflect:

How can you increase your knowledge of Jesus?

In what ways has your love for others blossomed as your friendship with Jesus becomes richer?

_____

_____

_____

_____

_____

_____

_____

_____

_____

_____

_____

_____

_____

_____

_____

Pray:

God, the more I know of You—as I experience Your good plan for me and Your love in spite of my failings—the more I love and trust You. Help me see others through the lens of Your love. Amen.

Bible Study Topic:
SANCTIFIED

Read: Acts 26; 1 Peter 1:13-25

Key Scripture:

"Open their eyes, so that they may turn from darkness to light and from the power of Satan to God, that they may receive forgiveness of sins and a place among those who are sanctified by faith in me."

Acts 26:18 ESV

Life Application:

We've been sanctified! Marked as holy. Set aside for divine use. He brought us out of darkness into the scouring light of His forgiveness and purpose for our lives. Jesus freed us from the oppressive power of the devil.

Reflect:

What does it mean to be holy?

Have you fully grasped that being saved is only step one, that God has a specific mission for your life?

_____

_____

_____

_____

_____

_____

_____

_____

_____

_____

_____

_____

_____

Pray:

Lord, prepare my mind for action. Keep me alert to the devil's schemes. Wipe away the desires that controlled me before I knew You. I desire to be holy in everything I do, just as You are holy. Thank You for sanctifying me. Amen.

Bible Study Topic:
COMMANDED TO LOVE

Read: MARK 12:28–34

Key Scripture:

" 'Love the Lord your God with all your heart and with all your soul and with all your mind and with all your strength.' The second is this: 'Love your neighbor as yourself.' There is no commandment greater than these."

MARK 12:30–31 NIV

Life Application:

Jesus' command to His followers is elegant in its simplicity. No lists of difficult-to-remember rituals and/or special words. Love—that's all He asks of believers. With everything we are, love God and one another.

Reflect:

Have you loved your neighbor today? This week? This month?

In what ways could you show love to your neighbor?

_____

_____

_____

_____

_____

_____

_____

_____

_____

_____

_____

_____

_____

_____

_____

Pray:

Lord, please show me the places in my heart where I have set up idols. Show me where my soul, mind, and strength are not being used fully for Your purposes. Fill my heart with love for You and those around me. Amen.

Bible Study Topic:
ABIDE IN HIM

Read: JOHN 15

Key Scripture:

"I am the vine; you are the branches. Whoever abides in me and I in him, he it is that bears much fruit, for apart from me you can do nothing."
JOHN 15:5 ESV

Life Application:

In nature, the vine supplies life to its branches. When cut off from the nourishment of the vine, the branch withers. Jesus said if we abide—remain, be present, endure, be held, kept—in Him, He will sustain us.

Reflect:

Are you trying to accomplish anything apart from the vine of Jesus right now?

Which definition of *abide* is most meaningful to you?

_____

_____

_____

_____

_____

_____

_____

_____

_____

_____

_____

_____

_____

_____

Pray:

Lord Jesus, You are the source of life. Help me abide in You instead of struggling to do things in my own power, outside of You. Instead, Lord, You promise that I can be held and kept if I remain with You. Amen.

Bible Study Topic:
BOLD WITNESS

Read: 2 Timothy 1–2

Key Scripture:

For God gave us a spirit not of fear but of power and love and self-control.
2 Timothy 1:7 ESV

Life Application:

Instead of thinking of this verse in the negative—don't fear—focus on what Paul says to pick up—power, love, and self-control. At the end of his life, Paul's message was "Don't be ashamed of Jesus! Keep your witness pure."

Reflect:

How often in life do you operate out of fear?

What might change if you shifted your focus to the power, love, and self-control we have from the Spirit?

_____

_____

_____

_____

_____

_____

_____

_____

_____

_____

_____

_____

_____

_____

_____

Pray:

God, how easily I forget that You have power over everything. Why should I fear what others will think or do because I love Jesus? Remake my life into one of power, love, and self-control. Amen.

Bible Study Topic:
SECRET TO RADIANCE

Read: Psalm 34

Key Scripture:

Those who look to him are radiant, and their faces shall never be ashamed.
Psalm 34:5 ESV

Life Application:

How many skin creams have you applied that promise glowing skin? Forget the cosmetics.
God says to look to Him, and your shame will be cleansed by the blood of Jesus' sacrifice.
You will be radiant before Him.

Reflect:

Have you struggled with regret and shame over your past, even after coming to Christ?
In what way can you claim this promise of radiant freedom from shame in your life?

_____

_____

_____

_____

_____

_____

_____

_____

_____

_____

_____

_____

_____

_____

Pray:

Jesus, You have forgiven my sins! Like the woman You encountered at the well who was living in immorality and shame, let my joy shine from my face. I never have to be ashamed again. Thank You, Jesus. Amen.

Bible Study Topic:
JESUS IS THE LIFE

Read: John 11:1-44

Key Scripture:

"I am the resurrection and the life. He who believes in me will live, even though he dies."
John 11:25 NIV

Life Application:

Martha's brother was dead, and Jesus didn't show. When He did come, Jesus didn't ease her grief with what He could do, He told her who He is—life. We can't always see what God is doing, but we can always trust who He is.

Reflect:

Have you, like Martha, ever questioned where God was during your devastation?

Can you trust that life is a person—Jesus—and you can have Him just by asking?

_____

_____

_____

_____

_____

_____

_____

_____

_____

_____

_____

_____

_____

_____

Pray:

Lord Jesus, Remind me that life is not my job, a religion, a hobby, or even my family. You are life itself. Please come into my reality—my pain and my joy—and open my heart to abundant life in You. Amen.

Bible Study Topic:
DON'T UNDERESTIMATE GOD

Read: ROMANS 4

Key Scripture:

God in whom he believed, who gives life to the dead and calls into existence the things that do not exist.

ROMANS 4:17 ESV

Life Application:

God is the giver of life and the creator of all things. There is nothing He cannot do. Our human limitations don't apply. Have faith through the cold, shadowed valleys, because God can bring what doesn't now exist into being.

Reflect:

Have you ever expected too little of God?

Is there an area in your life where you need to believe and have faith that God can change your reality?

_____

_____

_____

_____

_____

_____

_____

_____

_____

_____

_____

_____

_____

_____

Pray:

God, You are a game changer. You promised Abraham the impossible—his wife, too old to bear children, would give birth to a son who would become a nation. And it came to pass! Father, keep the truth before me that You are God. Amen.

Bible Study Topic:
FAITH PLUS

Read: 2 Peter 1

Key Scripture:

Make every effort to add to your faith goodness; and to goodness, knowledge; and to knowledge, self-control; and to self-control, perseverance; and to perseverance, godliness; and to godliness, mutual affection; and to mutual affection, love.

2 Peter 1:5-7 NIV

Life Application:

The fruit of these virtues—goodness, knowledge, self-control, perseverance, godliness, and love—bolster our effectiveness in God's Kingdom. Faith plus virtue keeps us from stumbling into Satan's traps.

Reflect:

In addition to professed faith in Jesus, do you exhibit any of these virtues in your life? How can these traits save us from stumbling?

_____

_____

_____

_____

_____

_____

_____

_____

_____

_____

_____

_____

_____

_____

Pray:

Lord Jesus, I say that I love You, but I also want to "make every effort to confirm my calling and election," as 2 Peter says. Help me walk without stumbling so I can lead others to You. Amen.

Bible Study Topic:
HIDDEN RICHES

Read: 2 Corinthians 6

Key Scripture:

Having nothing, and yet possessing everything.
2 Corinthians 6:10 NIV

Life Application:

Stuff is nice. It can pave life's potholes sometimes. But as followers of Christ, our focus lies in another place—the life to come. Even the poorest here on earth can be rich beyond measure with Christ.

Reflect:

Is your focus on accumulating possessions here on earth?

In what ways could you lay up treasures in heaven instead of on earth?

_____

_____

_____

_____

_____

_____

_____

_____

_____

_____

_____

_____

_____

_____

_____

Pray:

God, Your Kingdom isn't governed by the same standards as this world. In Your eyes the least shall be the greatest. Change my focus from gaining riches for myself to showing Your love to the world. Amen.

Bible Study Topic:
CHILDREN OF LIGHT

Read: EPHESIANS 5

Key Scripture:

For you were once darkness, but now you are light in the Lord. Live as children of light (for the fruit of the light consists in all goodness, righteousness and truth). EPHESIANS 5:8-9 NIV

Life Application:

A spear of light penetrates the darkness. And we weren't merely swathed *in* the darkness, we *were* darkness. But thanks to Jesus, our hearts are no longer blackened with sin. Now we beam with floodlight intensity!

Reflect:

Does your life reflect the fruit of the light?

How does light act differently than darkness?

....

....

....

....

....

....

....

....

....

....

....

....

....

....

....

....

....

....

Pray:

Lord, You turned my darkness into light. The darkness conceals and breeds shame and death. But Your light shatters the veil and scatters the shadows. I am a child of light—of goodness, righteousness, and truth. Amen.

Bible Study Topic:
AN OBEDIENT HEART

Read: Proverbs 31:10-31

Key Scripture:

Charm is deceptive, and beauty is fleeting; but a woman who fears the Lord is to be praised. Proverbs 10:30 NIV

Life Application:

Insincere words, jaded lives masked by designer clothes, hopeless expressions painted over with cosmetics. A lot of despair can be concealed beneath a spit-shined veneer. But God looks into our hearts. He sees our devotion to Him.

Reflect:

Have you bought in to the world's glorification of youth and beauty?

Do you need to reshape your priorities so love and obedience to God come first?

_____

_____

_____

_____

_____

_____

_____

_____

_____

_____

_____

_____

_____

_____

_____

Pray:

Heavenly Father, the world values charm and beauty, no matter what lies beneath. But You want to be my first love. Fake words and a coiffed exterior don't impress You. Give me a yielded, obedient heart. Amen.

CONTINUE COLORING WITH
THESE SPECIAL EDITIONS. . .

Spiritual Refreshment for Women: Everyday Promises Coloring Book

Color your way to an inspired faith with the *Everyday Promises* coloring book. Forty-six unique images on quality stock will comfort and inspire through beautiful design, prayers, and scriptural promises. The backs of each generous 8x10 coloring page are left blank—perfect for coloring with crayons, colored pencils, and markers.

Paperback / 978-1-68322-104-3 / $9.99

Bible Promise Book® for Hope & Healing Coloring Book

Color your way through the promises of scripture with *The Bible Promise Book® for Hope and Healing*. Forty-six unique images on quality stock will comfort and inspire through beautiful design and hope-filled scripture selections. The backs of each generous 8x10 coloring page are left blank—perfect for coloring with crayons, colored pencils, and markers.

Paperback / 978-1-68322-105-0 / $9.99

Spiritual Refreshment for Women: Everyday Encouragement Coloring Book

Color your way to an inspired faith with the *Everyday Encouragement* coloring book. Forty-six unique images on quality stock will comfort and inspire through beautiful design and devotional-like thoughts and scripture selections. The backs of each generous 8x10 coloring page are left blank—perfect for coloring with crayons, colored pencils, and markers.

Paperback / 978-1-68322-102-9 / $9.99